PREFACE

As a Christian who was diagnosed with cancer in 2000, I know the struggle to think biblically when facing this dreaded enemy. And once the chemotherapy was over, I found that the battle continued on in a new way, a battle with fear in my mind. The fear was, "What if the cancer returns?"

Pastor Sensenig's reminders of biblical truths help to put thinking back on track. Section six on courage was especially helpful in battling fear.

— Kathleen Leach

Berean Bible Church
675 Lincoln Garden Road
Ephrata, PA 17522
(717) 733.6114
www.BereanInternetMinistry.org

Perfect bound and eBook editions available online
(Amazon, Barnes & Noble, etc.)

Perfect bound edition: 978-1-63073-148-9

eBook edition: 978-1-63073-149-6

Services provided by:
Faithful Life Publishers & Printers
North Fort Myers, FL 33903
888.720.0950
www.FaithfulLifePublishers.com

CANCER AND THE CHRISTIAN LIFE
(WORDS OF COMFORT & HOPE)

By Pastor Kelly Allen Sensenig

Over the years as a pastor, I have had many opportunities to comfort dear Christian people who have been suddenly diagnosed and afflicted with the disease of cancer. I have watched them as they sit on pins and needles awaiting the doctor's details about what type of cancer they have and how to treat the particular kind of cancer that has invaded their body. In some cases, Christian people whom I have known and served the Lord with for many years, had to face the challenge that they might not have much time left on earth. I have sat with people and sorrowed with them and have tried to enter into their world. But I knew that they needed something more and Someone bigger than myself to bring them through such a deep valley (Psalm 23:4). This is why I have repeatedly pointed them to the promises of God's Word and the person of our blessed Lord while they faced their difficult trial with cancer.

There is a very real fear and many new challenges that Christian brethren face as they deal with this life-changing disease. Because of this, I have been led to write some comforting, reassuring, and hopeful truths for those cancer patients in my church and other believers, who might benefit from the precious promises and comfort that the Scriptures bring to our hearts during times of trial.

Romans 15:4
"For whatsoever things were written aforetime were written for our learning, that we through patience and comfort of the scriptures might have hope."

Like most pastors, I try and give encouraging, helpful, and hope-filled words to those dear saints who have been diagnosed with cancer. But over the years, I have discovered that the comfort we receive only comes by looking into the eternal Word of God. It's here that we rediscover and reclaim the unchanging promises of God and those portions of Scripture that we can apply to our own personal lives which help us face times of personal crisis and hurt – even cancer.

Cancer does not seem to pick and choose whose body it's going to invade. It is a diagnosed disease among all walks of life - both adults and children, and Christians and non-Christians alike. It is not a friend to Christian people. But we must understand that the Christian can face cancer with a different outlook and attitude than the non-Christian or unsaved person who is not in touch with the living God. Believers can face this difficult disease with the reassurance that God is on their side and that God's promises can be a steady rock for them while they face cancer. Many books have been written on how we develop cancer in our bodies. But to my knowledge, little has been written concerning how the child of God can deal with cancer from a spiritual perspective.

Not long ago I was handed a little note that in a small way dealt with cancer from a spiritual perspective. The note came from a concerned wife whose own husband had been diagnosed with cancer. Everything was up in the air at this particular time of their lives. They were not sure what the future held physically or financially. The cancer had turned their lives in a totally different direction. But on this little piece of paper some anonymous author wrote down several points and promises about what cancer couldn't do to the Christian life. The unknown author entitled his or her thoughts this way – "What Cancer Can't Do."

I would like to take this title and the short points expressed on this paper and share them with you. However, I would like to take the time to expand these points with Scripture and various comments. I would also like to add several points of my own to those already expressed by this unknown author. May God be pleased to use these Scripture promises to help those who have been diagnosed with cancer and who are now suffering through the effects and treatments related to cancer.

WHAT CANCER CAN'T DO

1. CANCER CANNOT STOP THE HOLY SPIRIT'S MINISTRY IN YOUR LIFE.

> Jesus said in John 14:16:
> "And I will pray the Father, and he shall give you another Comforter (helper), that he may abide with you for ever."

The Holy Spirit is called the Comforter because He comes alongside of us to give us spiritual aid and consolation during times of difficulty.

The hymn writer, Doc M. Shanks, wrote these lovely words:

> "I'm rejoicing night and day,
> As I walk the pilgrim's way,

For the hand of God in all my life I see,
And the reason of my bliss,
Yes, the secret all is this: That the Comforter abides with me.

He abides, He abides, Hallelujah, He abides with me!
I'm rejoicing night and day,
As I walk the pilgrim way,
For the Comforter abides with me."

As a Christian, you must remember that cancer cannot take away the Spirit's abiding ministry in your heart and life. Jesus said that the Holy Spirit would have an indwelling and life-changing ministry that is unending ("for ever"). The Spirit is promised to be your helper ("Comforter") as He reveals the power and provision of Jesus Christ to your own personal life. Jesus promised that "I will come to you" (John 14:18) when speaking about the time when the Holy Spirit would take up a permanent residency in His followers. This obviously means that the Holy Spirit would reveal Christ's life to them and make Christ's indwelling life real and precious to His disciples ("Christ in you, the hope of glory" - Col. 1:27). Jesus also said in John 16:14 that "He (the Holy Spirit) shall glorify me: for he shall receive of mine, and shall shew *it* unto you."

How wonderful this is to contemplate! The Spirit's ministry is to reveal the glories and grandeur of the life of Jesus Christ to your own personal life. As you face various types of cancer, you can be sure that the Holy Spirit will be with you to reveal Christ to you and bring His comfort, strength, and help into your life, which is called "the supply of the Spirit of Jesus Christ" (Phil. 1:19). This is the Spirit's special ministry today. He wants to make the life of Jesus very personal and precious to your own life during the time of suffering. You can be sure that God will be with you through the abiding ministry of the Holy Spirit. Your body is "an habitation of God through the

Spirit" (Ephesians 2:22). God is with you, beside you, before you, behind you, below you, above you, and in you. Yes, God dwells in you through the Spirit's presence. As you face cancer you must remember that you will not face it alone!

> "On life's pathway I am never lonely,
> My Lord is with me, My Lord divine;
> Ever present Guide, I trust Him only,
> No longer lonely, for He is mine.
>
> No longer lonely, No longer lonely,
> For Jesus is the Friend of friends to me;
> No longer lonely, No longer lonely,
> For Jesus is the Friend of friends to me."
> — Robert Harkness

Hebrews 13:5:
"… for he hath said, I will never leave thee, nor forsake thee."

Psalm 46:1:
"God *is* our refuge and strength, a very present help in trouble."

Psalm 46:11:
"The LORD of hosts *is* with us; the God of Jacob *is* our refuge. Selah."

God cannot forsake His own children. He abides with His children forever and stays by their side. The Holy Spirit, who reveals the presence of God to you today, will help you during your time of cancer in every way imaginable. This is because the Holy Spirit will be your Helper or Comforter while facing your daily and hourly battle with cancer. He will help you *mentally* with the spiritual battles of your mind, *emotionally* as you experience a troubled heart, and also *physically* as you encounter new kinds of pain and discomfort. Cancer does not have to quench or extinguish the Spirit's ministry in your life (1 Thess. 5:19).

As we will see, the remaining points of this study are actually the results of the Spirit's ministry and work taking place within your own heart. But what is the goal of the Spirit's work in your life as you face your battle with cancer? Ultimately it is to help you become more like Christ.

2 Corinthians 3:18 says:
"But we all, with open face beholding as in a glass (mirror) the glory of the Lord (seeing Christ in our life!), are changed into the same image from glory to glory (one level of Christlikeness into another), *even* as by the Spirit of the Lord."

J. B. Phillips said: "Every time we say, 'I believe in the Holy Spirit,' we mean that we believe that there is a living God able and willing to enter human personality and change it."

The Holy Spirit will continually help you to become fashioned into the likeness of Jesus Christ as you pass through your battle with cancer and receive chemo treatments. The Holy Spirit will reveal Christ to you and through His fruitful ministry (Gal. 5:22-23) conform your life to the likeness of Jesus Christ.

Yes, it's the ministry of the Holy Spirit in our lives to reveal Christ to us – His power, provision and lovely person ("that I may know him" - Phil. 3:10). The reason for the working of the Spirit's ministry in your life is so you might develop a closer and more intimate relationship with Jesus Christ and become more like Christ in a greater way, as the Holy Spirit makes the person of Christ real to your own life – His patience, peace and power. Your cancer should change your life as the Spirit reveals Christ to you in a powerful and dynamic way. "The Spirit of life in Christ Jesus" (Romans 8:2) means that the Holy Spirit wants to introduce Jesus Christ to your own life and reveal Christ to you so that you might become more like Him.

> "All the way from earth to Glory,
> I would be like Jesus;
> Telling o'er and o'er the story,
> I would be like Jesus.
>
> Be like Jesus, this my song,
> In the home and in the throng;
> Be like Jesus, all day long!
> I would be like Jesus."
>
> — James Rowe

Beloved, don't allow your cancer to quench or stop the working ministry of the Holy Spirit in your heart. Instead, allow your cancer to increase the Spirit's work in your life. The Holy Spirit's ministry can continue to operate in your heart in a new and fresh way. You need the Spirit's ministry of comfort and strengthening grace during your bout with cancer. If you do not depend upon the Spirit's work in your heart and life, you will become a spiritual pauper as you face cancer. But if you depend upon His ministry in your time of suffering and affliction, you can experience the true riches ("spiritual blessings" – Ephesians 1:3), which you have in Christ, as the Holy Spirit reveals and unleashes these blessings in your daily living.

We are reminded in this first point that the Holy Spirit is both the Comforter and Conformer (John 16:13-14) who makes us more like Jesus Christ. Your prayer during this time of cancer should be: "Dear Lord, control and empower me by the Spirit's assistance. Change me into the likeness of Christ through the Spirit's ministry. Help me to see Thy beauty and grace. In Jesus' name, Amen."

In the words of the hymn writer, Daniel Iverson:

"Spirit of the living God,
Fall fresh on me.
Melt me, mold me, fill me, use me.
Spirit of the living God,
Fall fresh on me."

2. CANCER CANNOT CRIPPLE YOUR LOVE.

This is a pleasant reminder while you suffer with cancer. First, cancer cannot cripple the love that you have for the Lord. This is a love that will live on in your heart as you walk close to the Lord.

The Psalmist said in Psalm 18:1-2:
"I will love thee, O LORD, my strength. The LORD *is* my rock, and my fortress, and my deliverer; my God, my strength, in whom I will trust; my buckler, and the horn of my salvation, *and* my high tower."

Cancer cannot cripple your love relationship and fellowship that you have with the Lord. The nearness and dearness of God to your own heart cannot be lost as you pass through the deep waters with your trial of cancer. In fact, cancer should deepen your love relationship with the Lord. A new awareness of His divine presence should flood into your soul and you should grow closer to the Lord. Cancer cannot take away the love that you have developed and had with the Lord over the passing years. Cancer can only strengthen this relationship and bring you into a closer relationship with the precious Lord.

James 4:8 asks us to:
"Draw nigh to God, and he will draw nigh to you…"

Trials should cause you to inspect your relationship with God and ultimately draw you closer to the Lord. The cancer that you now have should be used as a springboard to deepen your walk and relationship with the Lord. This experience should bring a new awareness of God's presence into your life and reveal His earnest desire to fellowship with you on a daily basis and deeper level.

"Thou my everlasting portion,
More than friend or life to me,
All along my pilgrim journey,
Savior, let me walk with Thee.

Close to Thee, close to Thee,
Close to Thee, close to Thee;
All along my pilgrim journey,
Savior, let me walk with Thee."

— Fanny Crosby

Cancer cannot destroy your personal relationship with Jesus Christ. This is a comforting truth to know and experience. Paul said, "For to me to live is Christ" (Phil. 1:21). He did not say, "For me to live is cancer." Cancer cannot take away your love relationship with Jesus Christ. Your life must continually revolve around your personal love relationship with Jesus Christ. You can fellowship with the Lord in a deep and wonderful way as you face cancer.

The martyred Jim Elliot expressed fellowship with God in this way: "To stand by the shadows of a friendly tree with the wind tugging at your coattail and the heavens hailing your heart, to gaze and glory and to give oneself again to God, what more could a man ask? Oh, the fullness, pleasure, sheer excitement of knowing God on earth. I care not if I never raise my voice again for Him, if only I may love Him, please

Him. Mayhap (perhaps), in mercy, He shall give me a host of children that I may lead through the vast star fields to explore His delicacies whose fingers' ends set them to burning. But if not, if only I may see Him, smell His garments, and smile into my Lover's eyes, ah, then, not stars, nor children, shall matter--only Himself."

Psalm 42:1:
"As the hart (deer) panteth after the water brooks,
so panteth my soul after thee, O God."

"Wherever I go - only Thou!
Wherever I stand - only Thou!
Just Thou; again Thou!
Always Thou! Thou, Thou!
When things are good, Thou!
When things are bad - Thou!
Thou, Thou, Thou!"

Second, cancer cannot cripple the love that you have for other people. Your precious love for family and God's people cannot be taken away from your life. Cancer cannot kill loving friendships or memories that you have with other people.

Proverbs 17:17 reminds us that "A friend loveth at all times..." This is true even in the times of cancer. True friendships cannot be dissolved as you pass through cancer in this present life. God has given to you close family and Christian friends to encourage your heart and pray for you during your bout with cancer. This can become a tremendous uplift to your heart in times of desperation and need. Faithful friends are one of life's greatest assets.

A friend is:
"A push when you've stopped
A word when you're lonely

A guide when you're searching
A smile when you're sad
A song when you're glad."

Third, cancer cannot steal away your love for lost souls who are in need of the saving message of Jesus Christ. In fact, I have seen how many Christians with cancer have been given opportunities by the Lord to share their faith in Jesus Christ. Affliction brings new opportunities to share Christ with others such as nurses, doctors and those who are suffering with the same disease.

In 2 Corinthians 2:12, Paul said that when he came to Troas to preach the gospel: "… a door was opened unto me of the Lord." Cancer brings many open doors of witness where we can effectively share Christ with the lost. We can reach people that we could not reach before.

"Lord, teach me how to love and live
That I may cheer each heart,
And to my fellowman in need
Some blessing rich impart."

As a cancer patient, you must view cancer as an open door to reach others for Christ. This will put a new perspective on your time of suffering. You have the Gospel blessing that you can share with others.

Will Houghton wrote:
"Lead me to some soul today,
O teach me, Lord, just what to say;
Friends of mine are lost in sin,
And cannot find their way.
Few there are who seem to care,
And few there are who pray;
Melt my heart, and fill my life,
Give me one soul today."

Fourth, cancer can allow you to have a loving and compassionate ministry with other believers in Christ who are passing through the same kind of trial that you are facing. As a fellow Christian, you can comfort them through writing a letter, speaking with them over the phone, or perhaps meeting them in person.

2 Corinthians 1:4 reminds us of the purpose of God's comfort:

"Who comforteth us in all our tribulation, that we may be able to comfort them which are in any trouble, by the comfort wherewith we ourselves are comforted of God."

The words of Joseph Parker can be applied to your life as you seek to comfort others who have the same disease as you: "Preach to the suffering, and you will never lack a congregation. There is a broken heart in every pew."

> "Out in the highways and byways of life,
> Many are weary and sad;
> Carry the sunshine where darkness is rife,
> Making the sorrowing glad.
>
> Make me a blessing, make me a blessing,
> Out of my life may Jesus shine;
> Make me a blessing, O Savior, I pray,
> Make me a blessing to someone today."
> — Ira B. Wilson

3. CANCER CANNOT STEAL AWAY THE JOY IN YOUR HEART.

Philippians 4:4:
"Rejoice in the Lord alway: *and* again I say, Rejoice."

Joy is not dependent on outward circumstances. Real joy cannot be stolen away by the cancer that has invaded your body. True inner joy is not dependent upon cancer. The Bible says that you can always rejoice or experience joy in the Lord. This means that joy comes from having a right relationship with God. Joy comes from keeping your eyes on the Lord and focusing on His person and wonderful abiding presence in your life. Let's be realistic. You are not rejoicing over the fact that you were diagnosed with cancer. But in the midst of the cancer you can rejoice in the Lord. What a difference this can make in your life! You can have joy even when the tears are flowing down your cheeks. This is because joy comes from the inside. You can rejoice in the Lord, His presence and personal care over your life, even when you are not rejoicing in the circumstances that are surrounding your life at this particular time. This is because joy comes from your close walk and relationship with the Lord and is not some kind of phony outward display of emotion or happiness.

Tim Hansel said: "Happiness is a feeling. Joy is an attitude. A posture. A position. A place."

Of course, this place of joy is found only in a loving, fulfilling and satisfying relationship with God. When you learn to rejoice in the Lord, the circumstances that surround your life, even cancer, cannot destroy your inner joy.

Paul said in 1 Thessalonians 1:6:
"And ye became followers of us, and of the Lord, having received the word in much affliction, with joy of the Holy Ghost:"

Like the Thessalonian believers, you can have God's inner joy even in the times of affliction and testing. This is because joy is not dependent upon your outward circumstances or surroundings. It is not based upon your physical condition or predicament in life. Cancer cannot steal away our joy. Peter reminds us that we can "rejoice with joy unspeakable and full of glory" (1 Peter 1:8). This means words cannot describe the inner joy and praise that God can give to us in times of distress and difficulty.

Haydn, the great musician, was once asked why his church music was so cheerful, and he replied: "When I think upon God, my heart is so full of joy that the notes dance and leap, as it were, from my pen, and since God has given me a cheerful heart it will be pardoned me that I serve Him with a cheerful spirit."

Psalm 32:11:
"Be glad in the LORD, and rejoice, ye righteous:
and shout for joy, all *ye that are* upright in heart."

Many years ago I sang these words in a music group. The words are true of the Christian life of inner joy.

> "Always there is music
> Always there is singing
> Always there is gladness
> In my heart since Christ has saved me!"

4. CANCER CANNOT DESTROY YOUR PEACE.

Sometimes you might become discouraged and distraught at what the cancer is doing on the inside of you, as it tries to invade your body and overtake your vital organs and interrupt your normal pattern of living. But dear brother or sister, let me remind you today that there is something that cancer cannot eat away or destroy. It is your inner peace that comes from the presence of the Lord. This is a reassuring promise that you can claim today even as you wade through the deep waters and the raging storm of cancer.

Jesus promised in John 14:27:
"Peace I leave with you, my peace I give unto you: not as the world giveth, give I unto you. Let not your heart be troubled, neither let it be afraid."

The peace that Jesus gives is "not as the world giveth" which means that His peace which He grants to His children is of a different nature than the world's offer of peace. The world of lost humanity looks at peace as something that we can have when everything is going our way and when our bank account is full. The world's peace is centered on cooperating circumstances whereas the Lord's peace is centered on Jesus Christ and our personal relationship with Him. It's a peace that can be possessed even when you know cancer has invaded your body. The peace of Jesus Christ can be yours even as you pass through your trial with cancer.

"Drop thy still dews of quietness,
Till all our strivings cease;
Take from our souls the strain and stress,
And let our ordered lives confess
The beauty of thy peace."

— John Greenleaf Whittier

Peace is an inner tranquility of soul that finds complete rest or calmness in God and His providence over our life. God said: "Be still and know that I am God" (Ps. 46:10) or relax and experience His stillness and peace.

Isaiah 26:3 records this similar promise:
"Thou wilt keep *him* in perfect peace, *whose* mind *is* stayed *on thee:* because he trusteth in thee."

Reflection or meditation upon the Lord's goodness, grace, mercy and beautiful person ("whose mind is stayed on thee") keeps our mind in a state of "perfect peace" and rest that the world without Christ cannot experience. It's a peace that we can possess in our hearts today when by faith ("because he trusteth in thee") we meditate upon God's plan, program, providence, and provision for our lives. It's through faith in God that we can experience His peace, inner tranquility, and stillness. Jesus gives peace in the midst of the storm.

"There is peace in the midst of my storm-tossed life
Oh there's an Anchor, there's a Rock to cast my faith upon.
Jesus rides in my vessel so I'll fear no alarm."

— Stephen Adams

Philippians 4:7:
"And the peace of God, which passeth all understanding, shall keep (guard) your hearts (from wrong feeling) and minds (from wrong thinking) through Christ Jesus."

God's peace "passeth all understanding" which means that its significance, blessing, and provision cannot be fully comprehended from a human perspective. Its depths are unfathomable and can never be fully exhausted. But the promise is sure; as a result of constant prayer and continual communion with the Lord, God's peace keeps us from experiencing debilitating fear and stops worry from invading our heart and destroying our life from a spiritual perspective. God's peace sets itself up as a military guard on the outside of the door of our heart so that worry and fear do not overtake our life. Daniel was able to spend the night with the lions in perfect peace!

Warren Wiersbe remarked that peace "does not mean the absence of trials on the outside, but it does mean a quiet confidence within, regardless of circumstances, people, or things." God's peace provides wonderful refreshment and hope.

"Like the sunshine after rain
Like a rest that follows pain
Like a hope returned again
Is the peace that Jesus gives.

Like the soft, refreshing dew,
Like a rosy day break new,
Like a friendship tender, true,
Is the peace that Jesus gives.

Oh the peace that Jesus gives
Never dies but only lives.
Like the music of a psalm
Like a glad eternal calm
Is the peace that Jesus gives
Is the peace that Jesus gives."
— Haldor Lillenas

5. CANCER CANNOT DIMINISH YOUR FAITH IN GOD.

Isaiah 26:4:
"Trust ye in the LORD for ever: for in the LORD JEHOVAH *is* everlasting strength."

"I trust in God wherever I may be,
Upon the land, or on the rolling sea,
For come what may, from day to day,
My heav'nly Father watches over me.

I trust in God, I know He cares for me;
On mountain bleak or on the stormy sea;
Though billows roll, He keeps my soul;
My heav'nly Father watches over me."
— William C. Martin

If your life has been rooted in the goodness and faithfulness of the Lord throughout the years, you can continue to possess great trust or faith in the Lord's power, provision and purpose for your life (Rom. 8:28), even as you pass through the deep waters of cancer.

> "Through it all, Through it all,
> Oh, I've learned to trust in Jesus;
> I've learned to trust in God.
> Through it all, through it all,
> Oh, I've learned to depend upon His Word."
>
> — Andraé Crouch

Faith not only looks at what God can do but also at what God does not do. It takes far greater faith to realize that you may not be completely healed from cancer and accept this condition as coming from the Lord. We must view faith at both ends of the spectrum. Sometimes God does choose to heal us while other times He chooses not to heal. Sometimes God answers our prayer in the way we pray while other times He answers in the way that He knows is best for our lives. We are reminded that our faith must continue to be built up and remain strong in the Lord and His providential plan over our lives.

Job 13:15 confidently says:
"Though he slay me, yet will I trust in him: but I will maintain mine own ways before him."

Erwin W. Lutzer remarked: "A Christian who walks by faith accepts all circumstances from God. He thanks God when everything goes good, when everything goes bad, and for the 'blues' somewhere in-between. He thanks God whether he feels like it or not."

Psalm 73:28 declares:
"But *it is* good for me to draw near to God: I have put my trust in the Lord GOD, that I may declare all thy works."

We can see the strong faith that the psalmist had in God. *Faith makes the way brighter and the load lighter.* This is the same kind of faith that you can possess as you pass through your own personal experience with cancer. You can know that He is the sovereign God who is in charge of the events of your life and as a result you can allow your faith to continually blossom within your heart.

Oswald Chambers once said: "It is a great thing to be a believer, but easy to misunderstand what the New Testament means by it. It is not that we believe Jesus Christ can do things, or that we believe in a plan of salvation. It is that we believe him; whatever happens we will hang on to the fact that he is true. If we say, 'I am going to believe he will put things right,' we shall lose our confidence when we see things go wrong."

"And Jesus answering saith unto them, Have faith in God" (Mark 11:22).

Dwight Lyman Moody said that there are three kinds of faith:

1. Struggling faith, like a man in deep water desperately swimming.

2. Clinging faith, like a man hanging to the side of a boat.

3. Resting faith, like a man safely within the boat (and able to reach out with a hand to help someone else get in). Proverbs 3:5-6:
   "Trust in the LORD with all thine heart; and lean not unto thine own understanding. In all thy ways acknowledge him (His will and purpose for your life), and he shall direct thy paths."

The Scriptures repeatedly ask you to trust in the Lord or have great faith in Him. God wants you to possess a heart that trusts in His plan and unfailing strength for your life. God is looking for your heart! You must learn to trust or have faith in His will and purpose for your life no matter what the details of God's purpose might include. If you practice living by faith you will not lean "unto thine own understanding" which simply means you will not rely upon your own wisdom, direction and will when facing some difficulty or hardship in life. Rather, as you face the many different situations and trials in life, including cancer, you must learn to "acknowledge him" which means to give consent to God's will and purpose and all-wise plan for your life. You must give God the right, or authority, to lead your life in every way that He has planned.

When you "acknowledge" God you are recognizing God's sovereignty over your life and are willing to step out in faith and follow His plan no matter what it might be. Only when you come to this place of surrender can God "direct thy paths" ("make straight your paths") in life, which means that God will show and confirm in your heart His perfect will and purpose for your life. God will cause you as a believer to rest in His will and providential plan for your life whatever that might involve. Cancer cannot diminish your faith if that faith is strong and rooted deeply in the sovereign workings of God. The Great Shepherd always inspects and approves the path that His sheep walk upon and "The LORD is my shepherd" (Ps. 23:1). Cast your faith upon God's providence and purpose for your life.

Helen Adams Keller once said: "Dark as my path may seem to others, I carry a magic light in my heart. Faith, the spiritual strong searchlight, illumines the way, and although sinister doubts lurk in the shadow, I walk unafraid toward the enchanted wood where the foliage is always green, where joy abides, where nightingales nest and sing, and where life and death are one in the presence of the Lord."

6. CANCER CANNOT OVERCOME YOUR COURAGE.

Joshua 1:9 says:
"Have not I commanded thee? Be strong and of a good courage; be not afraid, neither be thou dismayed: for the LORD thy God is with thee whithersoever thou goest."

Fear is one of the key battles that cancer patients face. I do not know this by experience, since I never had cancer, but I can verify that it is true. I have spoken with many dear saints over the years that have struggled with fear while going through various experiences with cancer. There is the fear of the cancer spreading, the fear of what lies in the future, the fear of reoccurring cancer, the fear of paying bills, and the fear of leaving loved ones behind to face life without your help. There are many fears that can overtake you as you face cancer. But remember that God can help you to overcome your fears so that they do not debilitate your life. Yes, it is human to experience fears but by God's divine help you do not have to allow these fears to control you, overtake your life, and ruin you from a spiritual standpoint. The promise of God's abiding presence will help you to "be strong and of a good courage."

I've always taught people to pray through verses that give personal promises of deliverance over the fears that are trying to haunt them. This is one way you can use the Bible as the "sword of the Spirit" (Ephesians 6:17) and effectively ward off Satan's attempts to bring fear into your life. Below are some verses you can pray through which will help you overcome fear in your life as you face cancer. Practice praying the Word of God and you will find great comfort and deliverance from overcoming fears.

Psalm 34:4:
"I sought the LORD, and he heard me, and delivered me from all my fears."

God's presence will always be available to sustain you. Someone said, "God, you are already there waiting for me tomorrow!"

Prayer: "Lord, I am coming to You in prayer and I know that You hear me today. Please deliver me from all my fears as I face this trial of cancer in my life. I need Your delivering power. In Jesus' name, Amen."

Psalm 118:6:
"The LORD *is* on my side; I will not fear: what can man do unto me?"

Isaiah 41:10:
"Fear thou not; for I *am* with thee: be not dismayed; for I *am* thy God: I will strengthen thee; yea, I will help thee; yea, I will uphold thee with the right hand of my righteousness."

Prayer: "Lord, I know that You are on my side. You have not forsaken me. Because of this, I know that I do not have to fear. I know that You are my God and will strengthen me, help me, and uphold me so that I do not have to be overcome with plaguing fears. In Jesus' name, Amen."

Romans 8:15:
"For ye have not received the spirit of bondage again to fear; but ye have received the Spirit of adoption, whereby we cry, Abba, Father."

2 Timothy 1:7:
"For God hath not given us the spirit of fear; but of power, and of love, and of a sound mind."

Take the time to look up more verses dealing with fear and write them down on a note card. Make them part of a daily routine of prayer as you face your battle with cancer. This will help you immensely.

Another Personal Prayer: "Thank You Lord that You have promised to deliver me from an inward spirit of fear. Lord, thank You for giving to me Your own power, love and this sound or disciplined mind, whereby I can experience deliverance from fear. Thank You for Your promised deliverance. I claim it today. In Jesus' name, Amen."

On this side of Heaven we will never completely rid our lives of fear, but we can be delivered from the type of fear that overcomes our lives, pulls us down spiritually, and robs us of our faith in the Lord's power, provision, and purpose. The presence of the Lord will help us to "be strong and of a good courage." God has promised deliverance from the debilitating effects of fear.

A large old Bible, frequently used by Abraham Lincoln during the critical years of the Civil War, falls open easily to the 34th Psalm. If you examine that page, you will note that it is smudged at one spot. It seems obvious that the long, tapering fingers of the great emancipator often rested heavily on the fourth verse, which reads: "I sought the Lord, and He heard me, and delivered me from all my fears." Lincoln had obviously come to realize that God is a mighty refuge. The awareness of the Lord's presence had undoubtedly garrisoned the President's heart during his most severe difficulties and trials.

John Newton said:
"How sweet the name of Jesus sounds
In a believer's ear!
It soothes his sorrows, heals his wounds,
And drives away his fear!"

7. CANCER CANNOT INVADE YOUR HEART.

2 Corinthians 4:16:
"For which cause we faint not; but though our outward man perish, yet the inward *man* is renewed day by day."

The outward man is our body and we can be sure that every one of us has a body that is moving in a downward direction. The second law of thermodynamics is true when it comes to our bodies. Everything breaks down in time and deteriorates. But you can be sure that the second law of thermodynamics does not apply to your inward spiritual life or your heart and soul which is the control center of your life. Cancer cannot invade the soul and destroy your inner life in any way. Your soul cannot get cancer.

This is wonderful reassurance! The inward control center of your life can continually be tuned in to God. You can walk with Him and experience inward strength and growth in your Christian life in the same manner that you always have throughout your previous days. Cancer cannot invade your inward fellowship with God, your spiritual communication with the Lord and the inner strength and joy that comes from walking with God. It can be summertime in your soul no matter what the outward cold winds of pain and cancer do to your body. What matters most in life is what happens *in* us, not *to* us!

The following story is about a handicapped high school student. Although the crutches on which he hobbled kept him from being physically active, he excelled in his studies and was well liked by his peers. They saw the problems he had getting around, and they sometimes felt sorry for him, but for a long time nobody asked him why he had this difficulty. One day, however, his closest friend finally did. "It was polio," answered the student. The friend responded, "With so many difficulties, how do you keep from becoming bitter?" Tapping his chest with his hand, the young man replied with a smile, "Oh, it never touched my heart."

Dear friend, cancer cannot touch your soul or heart. It cannot invade the inner life where God supplies you with a daily renewing of spiritual strength. The heart is the place where God provides you with a continual feast of joy, peace and fellowship with Himself during the valleys and wilderness journeys of your life (Ps. 23:4-5; 78:19). God desires to work on the inner man because this is where true spiritual life exists and where we must grow (2 Peter 3:18). It's here that the Holy Spirit changes the life of the believer from glory to glory (2 Cor. 3:18).

> Ephesians 3:16 says:
> "That he would grant you, according to the riches
> of his glory, to be strengthened with might by his
> Spirit in the inner man."

What is happening on the inside of your heart is more important than what cancer is doing on the inside of your body. You will notice that the text in 2 Corinthians 4:16 says "the inward *man* is renewed day by day" through the Lord's inner presence and work of strengthening and sustaining grace. While physically we might grow weaker, spiritually we can experience the inward renewing and growth of our soul. David said, "He restoreth my soul" (Psalm 23:3). What a marvelous promise and ever-present reality this can be in our lives today. Day by day we can experience this inward renewing of our soul. Our inward spiritual life can continue to blossom like a rose in a desert because of the Lord's inner work of grace taking place within our heart.

> "Day by day and with each passing moment,
> Strength I find to meet my trials here;
> Trusting in my Father's wise bestowment,
> I've no cause for worry or for fear,
>
> He whose heart is kind beyond all measure
> Gives unto each day what He deems best—
> Lovingly, its part of pain and pleasure,
> Mingling toil with peace and rest."
>
> — Lina Sandell Berg

8. CANCER CANNOT SILENCE YOUR WORSHIP AND THANKSGIVING BEFORE GOD.

Most of us are aware of the man in Scripture called Job. This man lost his family, fortune and fame. One would think that he would throw in the towel, curse God, and die. But this is not what Job did after facing his great calamities in life. In the midst of the plaguing events and problems that Job faced, we find that he worshipped God.

Job 1:20 records these words: "Then Job arose, and rent his mantle, and shaved his head, and fell down upon the ground, and worshipped." Wreckage in life should always cause us to worship God. Wreckage leads to worship. Trials should not drag us away from the Lord, but draw us closer to the Lord where we worship Him in newness and freshness of spirit.

Psalm 25:1:
"Unto thee, O Lord, do I lift up my soul."

Oh the beauty of lifting your soul up to the Lord in worship! Oh the beauty of opening your heart to Him and pouring out your soul to God. The Bible says that in the midst of life's trials we can be thankful and have a worshipping heart.

1 Thessalonians 5:18:
"In every thing give thanks: for this is the will of God in Christ Jesus concerning you."

One man said to me, "I thank God for cancer because it has drawn me closer to the Lord." His attitude reminds us that we can be thankful in the midst of every trial that we face in life and for the trials that God allows to come into our lives.

"And I thank You Lord, for the trials that come my way,
In surrender of everything, life is so worthwhile.
And I thank You Lord, that when everything's put in place,
Out in front I can see Your face and it's there You belong."

— Dan Burgess

You can always be thankful to the Lord and rejoice in the wonderful life and presence of the Lord during times of trial. You can always show gratitude for the wonderful things that He has done throughout your life and what He is doing in your life, even as you pass through the deep valley of cancer with all of its related pain and treatments. In the midst of the storm there can be a song of thanksgiving and worship. After all, we are to rejoice in the Lord and the beauty of His presence.

Let us look at Philippians 4:4 one more time:
"Rejoice in the Lord alway: *and* again I say, Rejoice."

We do not necessarily rejoice in the trying circumstances that we must face as a cancer patient. But we can rejoice in the beauty and wonder of God's person and the blessings of peace, joy and patience that He provides. There can be a song of worship and thanksgiving in our heart even in the midst of the storm. This is because the Christian finds thanksgiving, joy and a worshipful heart, not in the absence of danger and trial, but in the presence of God. Dear friend, it's through deep trials, such as cancer, that our ordinary worship can increase into a beautiful melody and symphony of praise.

Composer Don Wyrtzen told the true story of the great pianist Paderewski, who on one occasion was performing in Carnegie Hall. In the audience was a mother and her young son. During the intermission the woman suddenly realized that the boy was no longer at her side. Just then, over the voices of the milling crowd, she heard the distinct notes of "Chopsticks" being played on the piano. The child had found his way onto the stage and was sitting at the magnificent Steinway concert grand. A moment later lovely music could be heard. Paderewski had quietly slipped behind the youngster, placed his talented hands over the boy's and added a beautiful accompaniment to that simple tune.

In a similar way, the Lord wants to create the beautiful music of worship and thanksgiving in our hearts and lives during our trial with cancer. We must allow God to use our trials, such as cancer, to bring forth the sweet music of praise and glory unto the Lord. Hebrews 13:15 calls our worship "the sacrifice of praise to God continually…" Indeed, cancer cannot keep you from worshipping and praising the Lord. God actually uses trials to increase your praise, thanksgiving and worship of Him. In the midst of the darkness there is worship. God will give us songs in the night!

Job 35:10:
"But none saith, Where *is* God my maker, who giveth songs in the night."

Psalm 77:6:
"I call to remembrance my song in the night: I commune with mine own heart: and my spirit made diligent search."

> "Songs in the night,
> Songs in the night,
> The Lord giveth songs in the night;
> Sorrows may come,
> Days dark and drear,
> Still He giveth songs in the night."
>
> — Wendell Loveless

9. Cancer cannot shut out your past memories.

1 Thessalonians 1:3 says:
"Remembering without ceasing your work of faith, and labour of love, and patience of hope in our Lord Jesus Christ, in the sight of God and our Father."

Paul also said in Philippians 1:3:
"I thank my God upon every remembrance of you."

The old saying goes like this: "God gave us our memories so that we might have roses in December."

To remember the past is to see that we are here today by His grace and realize that every day and every relationship is a precious gift from God. Therefore, we should remember our family and all the friendships that we have enjoyed in the past and be thankful unto the Lord. Cancer cannot shut out your past memories with those people whom you love deeply. It cannot dissolve the wonderful years and experiences that you had together and the precious moments of life that you have shared together.

J. B. F. Wright wrote about the precious memories we have of beloved family and friends.

> "Precious memories, how they linger,
> How they ever flood my soul;
> In the stillness of the midnight,
> Precious, sacred scenes unfold.
>
> As I travel on life's pathway,
> Know not what the years may hold;
> As I ponder, hope grows fonder,
> Precious memories flood my soul."

Precious memories will continue to be part of your life even as you face cancer. This is a positive outlook that you can have as you deal with cancer. Like Paul, you can be thankful for memories and the wonderful times that God has given to you with family and friends. You can roll back the curtain of memory and praise the Lord for family and Christian friends that He has given to you and blessed your life with. Cancer cannot shut out these memories. Furthermore, recalling the past should give us a thankful heart in view of the blessings that God has showered upon our lives over the years with our family and Christian friends.

Someone has said: "You can't turn back the clock. But you can wind it up again."

10. CANCER CANNOT LESSEN THE POWER OF GOD'S GRACE.

The Bible gives the promise of sufficient grace. 2 Corinthians 12:9 has been a verse that many have claimed in the time of suffering and ailment. Who can forget what the Lord communicated to Paul when He said: "… My grace is sufficient for thee: for my strength is made perfect in weakness. Most gladly therefore will I rather glory in my infirmities, that the power of Christ may rest upon me."

We often talk about the sufficiency of God's strengthening and enabling grace but do we really believe in it? Have we really experienced it when the rubber meets the road?

2 Corinthians 3:5 reminds us:
"Not that we are sufficient of ourselves to think any thing as of ourselves; but our sufficiency *is* of God."

God has not always promised to give us answers but He has always promised to give us grace! God promises complete inward strength for every situation that we must face in life. This is the wonderful promise of God. In 2 Corinthians 12:10 Paul said, "for when I am weak, then am I strong." So in reality, you become stronger only when you become weaker. Only when we feel our insufficiency are we ready to experience God's sufficiency.

"When darkness veils his lovely face,
I rest on his unchanging grace;
When all around my soul gives way,
He then is all my hope and stay."
— Edward Mote

Vance Havner once said: "Jesus we all have; He is all we need and all we want. We are shipwrecked on God and stranded on omnipotence!"

John 1:16 says:
"And of his fulness have all we received, and grace
for grace."

The word "fulness" speaks of God's complete resource
of loving grace and kindness that is at our disposal. God's
strengthening grace is provided to us in a repetitive and
consecutive fashion much like the waves of the ocean
continually crash upon the shore. The waves of God's
sustaining grace continually meet all our spiritual needs in life.
Cancer cannot lessen the power of God's grace from working
in and through us. It cannot stop the ever-rolling waves of
God's grace from sustaining our lives.

"He giveth more grace when the burdens grow greater;
He sendeth more strength when the labors increase.
To added affliction He addeth His mercy;
To multiplied trials, His multiplied peace.
His love has no limit; His grace has no measure;
His power has no boundary known unto men;
For out of His infinite riches in Jesus,
He giveth, and giveth, and giveth again."

— Annie Johnson Flint

James 4:6 reminds us of this continuous flow of grace:
"But he giveth more grace…" God promises sufficient,
sustaining and strengthening grace to help in the time of
need. Who can forget the promise of Hebrews 4:16: "Let us
therefore come boldly unto the throne of grace, that we may
obtain mercy, and find grace to help in time of need."

Christianity is not a way out; it's a way through! And
God has promised us the grace that we need so that we
can pass through whatever life throws in our pathway. Yes,
we can even pass through the difficult experience of cancer

victoriously by receiving the fullness of God's unchanging and sufficient grace.

"Many times I'm tried and tested as I travel day by day;
Oft I meet with pain and sorrows, and there's trouble in the way,
But I have the sweet assurance that my soul the Lord will lead,
And in Him there is hope for every day.
Oh His grace is sufficient for me,
And His love is abundant and free;
And what joy fills my soul just to know, just to know
That His grace is sufficient for me!"

— Mosie Lister

11. CANCER CANNOT STOP JESUS FROM CARING FOR YOU.

1 Peter 5:7 says:
"Casting all your care upon him; for he careth for you."

These words are very short and to the point and yet they become very valuable to us as we face great mountains that seem insurmountable. How reassuring and comforting it is to know that Jesus cares for you and that He will take your burdens or anxieties upon Himself, so that you do not have to bear them. My dear friend, Jesus does care about you, and He is deeply concerned about your burdened heart that may be weighing you down today. Peter reminds us that through prayer we can cast our anxieties upon the Lord, so that we do not have to be overcome by them. Jesus is the burden bearer. God's shoulder will bear the burden of your heart. This is the promise of the Word of God. The great and mighty God cares about your burden that you have right now in your life and He wants you to cast it upon Him. He cares for you!

"Our God is far greater than words can make known,
Exalted and holy, He reigns on His throne.
In infinite splendor He rules over all;
Yet He feeds the poor sparrows, and He knows when they fall.

He rides the wild heavens, He strides thro' the seas;
The high mountains tremble to hear His decrees.
His voice with great thunderings sounds from above;
But to His own children He whispers His love.

His power is great and will ever endure,
His wisdom is peaceable, gentle, and pure.
But greater than all these glories I see,
Is the glorious promise that He cares for me."

— Jimmy Owens

Do not despair my beloved friend. Jesus cares!

Hebrews 4:15 says:
"For we have not an high priest which cannot be touched with the feeling of our infirmities; but was in all points tempted like as *we are, yet* without sin."

"In every pang that rends the heart,
The Man of Sorrows has a part."

— Michael Bruce

Because Jesus became a man and lived on this earth for thirty-three years, our Lord has shared our experiences and can therefore understand the testings which we endure. This does not mean that Jesus had cancer. Jesus did not inherit the direct effects of sin (death and disease) from the fallen race since He was sinless. What this text means is that Jesus experienced great trials and testings, the greatest being the cross, so that He can sympathize with us and understand the kind of trials that we pass through in life. He is the sympathizing Jesus.

"The great Physician now is near,
The sympathizing Jesus;
He speaks the drooping heart to cheer:
O hear the voice of Jesus.

Sweetest note in seraph song,
Sweetest name on mortal tongue,
Sweetest carol ever sung,
Jesus, blessed Jesus."

— William Hunter

Jesus does understand about human frailty and the heartaches that accompany our personal lives. And because He cares so much about you, He wants you to approach Him through prayer, so that He can help you by expressing His tender loving care and compassion in your life.

Psalm 103:13:
"Like as a father pitieth *his* children, *so* the LORD pitieth them that fear him."

Psalm 34:18 adds:
"The LORD *is* nigh unto them that are of a broken heart; and saveth such as be of a contrite (crushed) spirit."

"Does Jesus care when my heart is pained
Too deeply for mirth and song;
As the burdens press, and the cares distress,
And the way grows weary and long?

O yes, He cares; I know He cares,
His heart is touched with my grief;
When the days are weary, the long nights dreary,
I know my Savior cares."

— Frank E. Graeff

A younger lady that was somewhat handicapped gave one of my friends a paper sign with two straggly written words – "*Jesus Cares.*" These are the most comforting words you could ever read and experience in your life. My roommate at college hung that sign in his room his entire senior year to remind himself that Jesus does care about his deepest needs in life and is immensely concerned about him. Dear friend, Jesus wants to shower His loving care, compassion, and complete provision upon your life today. "The Lord is at hand" (Phil. 4:5). Jesus is near. He cares.

12. CANCER CANNOT HINDER GOD'S PURPOSE FOR YOUR LIFE.

Psalm 119:75 reads like this:
"I know, O LORD, that thy judgments are right,
and that thou in faithfulness hast afflicted me."

This verse has always been in the Bible! It's amazing how many Christians have missed it. The Psalmist knew that God was working out a plan in his life even when he suffered affliction. There was a fresh awareness of the sovereignty of God working in connection with his life and affliction. You too must learn the secret of resting in the providence and purpose of God for your life. You must see divine providence in all of your affliction. This is something that many Christians fail to understand. God's sovereign purpose cannot be thwarted but will come to pass just as God ordained.

Romans 8:28:
"And we know that all things work together for good to them that love God, to them who are the called according to *his* purpose."

The Bible reminds us that God is "working" or more literally *weaving* a plan together for our lives. Nothing happens by chance. Things just don't happen; they are ordained by God "who worketh all things after the counsel of his own will" (Eph. 1:11).

This is why Job could say:

"Naked came I out of my mother's womb, and naked shall I return thither: the LORD gave, and the LORD hath taken away; blessed be the name of the LORD. In all this Job sinned not, nor charged God foolishly" (Job 1:21-22).

Henry van Dyke said: "Happy and strong and brave shall we be — able to endure all things, and to do all things – if we believe that every day, every hour, every moment of our life is in God's hands."

Beloved, God never moves without purpose or plan. God is sovereign and this means that He is ultimately in control of everything that happens to our lives – even cancer. God's unfailing purpose will come to pass in our life just as He planned. Cancer does not overturn God's purpose for our lives. What we pass through in life is always according to the Lord's ordained blueprint and pattern. And we can know that when we are in the furnace of affliction, God keeps His hand on the thermostat, never allowing us to experience more than we can bear.

God's plan and promise in suffering can be seen in 1 Corinthians 10:13: "There hath no temptation taken you but such as is common to man (COMMON TRIALS): but God *is* faithful, who will not suffer you to be tempted above that ye are able (CONTROLLED PRESSURES); but will with the temptation also make a way to escape, that ye may be able to bear *it*" (CONQUERING GRACE).

God promises controlled pressure over the temptations that come from the devil (James 1:13). For example, many times the devil will try and tempt us to doubt God's goodness, love, generosity, kindness, and His power to get us through a time of difficulty or illness. It's during this time we must remember God's unfailing promise. *God promises that we will not be tested above what He has planned and what we can bear as His child.* The Lord keeps His hand on the thermostat which means He is in control over the temptations and trials that we face. Furthermore, God always provides a way to escape so that we might be able to bear our personal test or trial. In the area of suffering, many times the way of escape comes to us by showering His added grace and power upon our lives so that we "may be able to bear" our load of suffering. God will grant us His sufficient power and strength as we pass through the deep waters. The will of God will never lead us where the grace of God cannot keep us.

Satan wants to veil God's faithfulness to us during times of illness but God wants His children to see His faithfulness in the midst of their suffering. God always cares about His children and His tender-loving mercies and compassions can be experienced every day.

Lamentations 3:22-23:
"*It is of* the LORD's mercies that we are not consumed, because his compassions fail not. *They are* new every morning: great *is* thy faithfulness."

Faith in God's providence, plan, and spiritual provision during the time of suffering will keep us from being consumed or overcome in life. In fact, God's constant care and provision during times of suffering should result in believers worshipping God. Friend, "God is faithful" (1 Cor. 1:9) and He will meet all of your needs as you pass through your trial with cancer so that you can say along with Job, "blessed be the name of the LORD."

Rowland Bingham, founder of the Sudan Interior Mission, was once seriously injured in an automobile accident. He was rushed to a hospital in critical condition. The following day, when he regained consciousness, he asked the nurse what he was doing there. "Don't try to talk now, just rest," she replied. "You have been in an accident." "Accident!" exclaimed Dr. Bingham. "There are no accidents in the life of a Christian. This is just an incident in God's perfect leading."

Someone remarked: "There are no accidents in the Christian life, just appointments."

Job 23:13-14 declares:
"But he *is* in one *mind,* and who can turn him? and *what* his soul desireth, even *that* he doeth. For he performeth *the thing that is* appointed for me: and many such *things are* with him."

How wonderful to realize that, when everything seems out of control, we are reminded once again that God is in control! Job understood that God was in charge of all the events of his life. God always moves according to His sovereign plan and brings to pass His perfect will for our lives, no matter if that plan seems to stop us in our tracks. We must remember that the same God who orders our *steps* (Ps. 37:23) also orders our *stops* to accomplish His purpose for our life.

John Wesley traveled one day along a narrow road filled with ruts. His carriage soon became stuck in the mud. The delay especially disturbed him because he was eager to get to the next town where he was scheduled to preach. While some helpers tried to get the vehicle moving, another Christian came by. Wesley talked with him a moment and perceived that the poor fellow was deeply troubled. Asking why he was so distressed, he learned that because of crop failure, the man was almost destitute. "I haven't been able to get the money together to pay the rent," he said despairingly. "The landlord is ready to turn us out, and I don't know where to go with my wife and children." "How much do you owe?" Wesley inquired. He was told that 20 shillings would clear the debt. "Well," said Wesley, "I believe we can handle that. The Lord evidently wanted me to meet you." Taking the money from his wallet, he handed it to the man and said, "Here, go and be happy!" Then turning to his companions, he exclaimed, "Now I see why our carriage had to get stuck in the mud. Our steps were halted so that we might help that needy family."

When God does decide to stop us in life with an illness, such as cancer or some other disease, we must remember that God is still on the throne and we can draw closer to Him through our difficult situation (James 4:8). The devil might tempt us to think that God is no longer in control but we can be sure that the Lord is sovereign over all the events of this world and our own personal life. Nahum 1:3 states: "the LORD hath his way in the whirlwind and in the storm, and the clouds *are* the dust of his feet."

William Cowper described God's providence like this:
"God moves in a mysterious way,
His wonder to perform;
He plants His footsteps in the sea,
And rides upon the storm."

This immortal hymn ("God Moves in a Mysterious Way") has been a source of great comfort and blessing to God's people. Yet few know of the trying circumstances which led to its composition. The writer, William Cowper, had sunk to the depths of despair as the result of grief and disappointment. Finally one foggy night, in a state of depression, he called for a horse-drawn "taxi" and asked to be taken to London Bridge on the Thames River, intending to commit suicide. After driving around in the mist for 2 hours, the cabby reluctantly told his passenger he was lost. Disgusted by the delay, Cowper left the cab and determined to find his way on foot. Walking only a short distance, he discovered he was back at his own doorstep! They'd been going in circles. Immediately he recognized the restraining hand of the Lord in this providential turn of events. Convicted by the Spirit, he realized that the way out of his troubles was to look to God for help, not to jump into the river. As he cast his burden on the Savior, his heart was comforted. With tears of gratitude he sat down and penned these words which have strengthened thousands on the brink of despair:

> "God moves in a mysterious way
> His wonders to perform;
> He plants his footsteps in the sea,
> And rides upon the storm.
> Ye fearful saints, fresh courage take;
> The clouds ye so much dread
> Are big with mercy, and shall break
> In blessings on your head."

—William Cowper

Beloved, do not doubt God's providence over your life as you face cancer. Don't lose sight of how God can use cancer for your own spiritual benefit and good (Rom. 8:28). Only when you place faith in God's sovereignty and purpose for your life can you find His peace, joy, sufficiency, and blessing.

13. CANCER CANNOT STOP YOU FROM GROWING IN YOUR CHRISTIAN LIFE.

Trials such as cancer should not cause you to become bitter, but better. Through it all we should emerge as a better and stronger saint who has grown in his character, walk and relationship with the Lord. *We must remember that God does not always change the circumstances, but He may often change us!* God wants us to be more like His Son (2 Cor. 3:18). Suffering should help us become more like Jesus by strengthening our faith and increasing our love, joy, peace, and patience, along with many other Christian virtues. We are pruned by God during times of suffering so we might grow and bear "fruit," "more fruit" (John 15:2) and "much fruit" (John 15:5). Cancer may stop your physical body from functioning as it should, but you can be sure that this disease cannot stop God's spiritual fruit from increasing in your life. Cancer does not need to affect your spiritual growth. In fact, the presence of trials, such as cancer, should cause you to grow even more and bear much spiritual fruit in your life. Growth flows out of suffering.

1 Peter 5:10 declares:

"But the God of all grace, who hath called us unto his eternal glory by Christ Jesus, after that ye have suffered a while, make you perfect, stablish, strengthen, settle *you.*"

You will notice how Peter said "after" you suffer for a while that you will find yourself reaching the goal of spiritual maturity ("perfect"). Through suffering, God is making you what you ought to be. He is completing or perfecting your life in a greater way. It's only "after" you suffer that you will find yourself becoming more stable and strong ("stablish" & "strengthen") and find yourself established ("settle") in your

Christian life and walk in a greater way. Suffering is for your good and you can be sure that cancer cannot stop spiritual growth from occurring in your life, since the suffering that God allows to come into your life should produce greater fruit and maturity.

The mother eagle teaches her little ones to fly by making their nest so uncomfortable that they are forced to leave it and commit themselves to the unknown world of air outside. God will sometimes do the same thing to us. He stirs up our comfortable nest in life, pushes us over the edge, and we are forced to use our wings to save ourselves from fatal falling. Read your trials in this light, and see if you cannot begin to get a glimpse of their intended purpose and meaning. Your wings are being developed. Growth or development is taking place.

Job 23:10:
"But he knoweth the way that I take: *when* he hath tried me, I shall come forth as gold."

Yes, God knows. God knows because He has ordained and ordered your time of suffering. Job describes the hardness and difficulty of his trial. And yet, he says that in the end he would be a better Christian for passing through the fiery trial. Your suffering with cancer is compared to a fiery furnace that removes the dross and refines the gold. Job knows that the suffering, pain and disappointment which trials bring will remove from his life those things that are not pure. In the end, when he has passed through the fiery trial, he would be much purer and refined as God's saint, even as gold that passes through the fire. Dear Christian, the trial of cancer should not keep you from growing but actually purify you and make you more Christlike in the end.

1 Peter 1:7 also speaks about the gold:
"That the trial of your faith, being much more precious than of gold that perisheth, though it be tried with fire, might be found unto praise and honour and glory at the appearing of Jesus Christ."

Our faith is put through the fiery test today so that in the future, when we stand before Jesus, it might be found stronger and more pure, resulting in Christ getting the praise for what He has accomplished in our life. *The fire is not designed to burn us out but to purify us for the future when we meet Jesus.* Trials change us for the good as we accept them from the Lord. They make us better Christians by causing a growth spurt to take place in our lives.

It's amazing how a single event can awaken within us a stranger totally unknown to us. It can bring about a person that is more spiritual and complete as a result of great trial. God is looking for the gold that comes from those Christians that suffer with cancer. And we must remember that all of our suffering comes into our lives because God loves us and wants to change us. Yes, God loves us the way we are, but He also loves us too much to leave us the way that we are! He wants to see us grow into greater Christlikeness (Rom. 8:29) as we pass through the fiery trial of suffering.

Charles Haddon Spurgeon said: "I am certain that I never did grow in grace one-half so much anywhere as I have upon the bed of pain."

"God never moves without purpose or plan
When trying His servant and molding a man.
Give thanks to the Lord though your testing seems long;
In darkness He giveth a song.

Now I can see testing comes from above;
God strengthens His children and purges in love.
My Father knows best, and I trust in His care;
Through purging more fruit I will bear.

O rejoice in the Lord, He makes no mistake.
He knoweth the end of each path that I take.
For when I am tried and purified,
I shall come forth as gold."
— Ron Hamilton

14. CANCER CANNOT SHATTER YOUR FUTURE HOPE.

Hope is our positive outlook for the future. The Biblical view of hope is not uncertainty or cynicism but complete confidence in what God has promised. Some people will use the word hope in a pessimistic manner by saying, "I hope that it will all pan out in the end and be true." However, the Bible describes the word hope as something that is confident and sure so each believer can say, "I can't wait for I know it is all true!"

First, cancer cannot shatter your confidence in the imminent (any moment) return of Christ and the ever-present hope of receiving a new body.

Philippians 3:20-21 says:

"For our conversation (citizenship) is in heaven; from whence also we look for the Saviour, the Lord Jesus Christ: Who shall change our vile body, that it may be fashioned like unto his glorious body, according to the working whereby he is able even to subdue all things unto himself."

"Someday, all pain and sorrow will erase,
Someday I'll see my Savior face to face,
Someday He is coming back for me!"

You will not have cancer forever! You can be sure of this! Even if your cancer is not totally cured in this life, you can be sure that it will be cured when you receive your new glorified and eternal body at the coming of Jesus Christ. Someday, and it may be today, you will receive a body just like Jesus Christ possessed when He rose from the grave. Think of it, my friend. Someday you will receive a new body no longer subject to pain, cancer, sin or any earthly sorrow. It will be a body that will never die. It will be a perfect, immortal body that you will enjoy throughout the ages of eternity.

A newsboy, thinly clad and drenched by the soaking rain, stood shivering in a doorway one cold day in November. He was trying hard to stay warm. Every few minutes his shrill cry could be heard, "Morning paper! Morning paper!" A man who was well protected by his coat and umbrella stopped to buy the early edition. Noting the boy's discomfort, he said, "This kind of weather is pretty hard on you, isn't it?" Looking up with a smile, the youngster replied, "I don't mind too much, Mister. The sun will shine again."

This is also true for the Christian who is suffering with cancer. The sun will shine again, if not in this life, then the next life. The gloom and rain of hardship that is associated with the decline of our physical body might prevail "for a season" (1 Peter 1:6), but the future promise of a new glorified body gives us the blessed hope of a brighter day of sunshine and gladness in terms of our physical health. The sun will shine again! The clouds will one day break and we will receive a new body that will never die or experience pain and sorrow again. What a hope we have as a born-again Christian.

Titus 2:13 says:
"Looking for that blessed hope, and the glorious appearing of the great God and our Saviour Jesus Christ."

The blessed hope of Christ's imminent return should become a living reality and hope that permeates our hearts when suffering with cancer or any other ailment. We must keep looking up! Jesus is coming again. Our redemption draweth nigh! Cancer cannot touch the blessed hope that we have in Christ's return and the ever-present reality of possessing a new body that is free from all physical disease and pain.

2 Corinthians 4:17-18:
"For our light affliction, which is but for a moment, worketh for us a far more exceeding *and* eternal weight of glory; While we look not at the things which are seen, but at the things which are not seen: for the things which are seen *are* temporal; but the things which are not seen *are* eternal."

Your affliction with cancer must be put in its proper perspective in relation to time, eternity and the future glory of the new body that you will receive someday when Jesus Christ returns. Your future destiny as a believer is one of great glory and splendor. The best is yet to come! If you compare the wondrous future glory to your present earthly battle with cancer, your cancer is seen to be a "light" (easy) and "temporal" (momentary) trouble during your time on earth. This does not mean that cancer is not a difficult trial to bear or pass through in this life. What it means is that we must learn to view cancer and all of our trials from an eternal perspective. The affliction by itself may seem heavy, but when viewed from the eternal perspective, or compared to your glorious destiny that awaits you, cancer is a very small, insignificant, and transitory trial.

As we look forward to the "weight" (degree or abundance) of the glory and splendor that we will someday enter, it makes our present day trials seem small and insignificant. In other words, the degree of suffering in our present life does not compare with the degree of glory and great blessing that awaits us in the future, when we receive our magnificent body of redemption with its release from all pain and sickness. We need to possess a proper perspective on eternity and the wonderful destiny that awaits us.

Romans 8:18 reveals something similar:
"For I reckon that the sufferings of this present time *are* not worthy *to be compared* with the glory which shall be revealed in us."

Paul is teaching that there can be no comparison between our present-day suffering and the future of our glorious inheritance, or the time when we receive our glorified and eternal body that possesses no cancer, pain, and suffering. The future is so much more glorious when compared to our present suffering that we can't begin to compare or measure the two intensity levels. The future glory far outweighs the present troubles that we are passing through. Keeping this eternal perspective will enable us to pass through our trials victoriously. Knowing what is going to take place in the future helps us to deal with the trials that we are facing today.

Look at the contrasts that we have seen in these two verses:
• Light affliction .... Eternal weight of glory
• Moment ....Eternal
• Things which are seen ....Things which are not seen
   (present hardships) .... (future blessings)
• Temporal .... The glory
   (difficulties in this life) .... (splendors of the next life)
• Present time...........................What shall be revealed in us
   (afflictions)...............................(perfect & painless body)

An anonymous poet put it like this:

"One little hour of watching for the Master,
Eternal years to walk with Him in white;
One little hour to bravely meet life's duties,
Eternal years to reign with Him in light.
One little hour for weary toils and trials,
Eternal years for calm and peaceful rest."

Second, cancer cannot shatter the hope of your future inheritance in Heaven.

As John and Betty Stam, early missionaries to China, were led to certain execution by their communist captors, someone asked, "Where are you going?" After saying he didn't know where the guards were going, John added, "But we're going to heaven."

1 Peter 1:3-4 gives us this promise:
"Blessed *be* the God and Father of our Lord Jesus Christ, which according to his abundant mercy hath begotten us again unto a lively hope by the resurrection of Jesus Christ from the dead, To an inheritance incorruptible, and undefiled, and that fadeth not away, reserved in heaven for you."

Peter promises that God's saints have been born again ("begotten") by the mercy of the Lord. As a result of this new birth we can develop a "lively hope" or "living hope" that stems from the resurrection of Jesus Christ. You will notice that this is called a "living hope" which means that it is designed to impact our life on a daily basis. Doctrine must get into our daily living. Because Jesus rose from the dead we can possess the DAILY HOPE that we too will live on throughout eternity in Heaven. Our future heavenly inheritance is *unchanging* ("incorruptible"), *unblemished* ("undefiled"), *unending* ("fadeth not away"), and *untouched* ("reserved in heaven for you"). This last word means that our place in Heaven is guarded for us. It will be there when we get there!

Our future heavenly destiny should be a confident hope ("living hope") that fills our hearts with great joy, peace, and anticipation as we walk this pilgrim pathway. As you experience various kinds of cancer, which seeks to invade and overtake your body, you can be sure of your eternal destiny in Heaven.

"And just think of stepping on shore and finding it Heaven,
Of taking a hand and finding it God's,
Of breathing new air and finding it celestial,
Of waking up in glory and finding it home."

— L. E. Singer

A little girl was taking an evening walk with her father. Wonderingly, she looked up at the stars and exclaimed: "Oh, Daddy, if the wrong side of heaven is so beautiful, what must the right side be!"

Dear Christian friend, we are going to a better place! The better land is Heaven and the half has not been told of the wondrous glories and joys that await us in this beautiful place! Cancer cannot steal this hope from our hearts, since we have the promise found in God's Word that our inheritance in Heaven will be there waiting for us as soon as we pass from this side of glory into the next.

A little boy got on the elevator in the Empire State Building in New York City. He and his daddy started to the top. The boy watched the signs flashing as they went by the floors: 10, 20, 30, 40, 50, 60, 70. They kept going, and he got nervous. He took his daddy's hand and said, "Daddy, does God know we're coming?"

Yes, God knows we are coming! He has a place already prepared for us. Jesus said, "I go to prepare a place for you" (John 14:2). Heaven is a prepared place for prepared people. What a living hope! While we suffer with cancer and other trials, we can have the absolute assurance that we are going to Heaven someday. There is something that cancer cannot shatter – hope. You can know that you are going to Heaven someday and that you will "dwell in the house of the LORD for ever" (Psalm 23:6).

> "Precious Lord, take my hand,
> Lead me on, let me stand,
> I am tired, I am weak, I am worn;
> Through the storm, through the night,
> Lead me on to the light:
> Take my hand, precious Lord,
> Lead me home."
>
> — Thomas A. Dorsey

15. CANCER CANNOT REDUCE ETERNAL LIFE.

This is the promise that Jesus gives to each one of us today who are God's born-again children. Jesus taught that every person must be "born again" (John 3:7) in order to receive a new way of life and possess eternal life, which is contrasted to eternal death or separation from God in hell.

John 3:16:
"For God so loved the world, that he gave his only begotten Son, that whosoever believeth in him should not perish, but have everlasting life."

John 6:47:
"Verily, verily, I say unto you, He that believeth on me hath everlasting life."

Jesus taught that He alone gives eternal life and it is based upon our belief or faith in Him (His death and resurrection). First, eternal or everlasting life speaks of a new birth that we receive the moment we believe on Jesus, which results in God granting us spiritual life that will never end. Eternal life is something that we can possess at this very moment ("hath everlasting life") if we have personally believed on Christ to be our Savior from hell. Elsewhere Jesus said, "He that believeth on the Son hath everlasting life: and he that believeth not the Son shall not see life; but the wrath of God abideth on him" (John 3:36).

Second, the eternal life which we already possess will continue to exist after our physical death occurs. Our eternal, spiritual life will be experienced in the unending joy and glory that we share with Christ in Heaven. Those who possess eternal life are given the wonderful promise "to be absent from the body, and to be present with the Lord" (2 Cor. 5:8).

Friend, you may be a hurting cancer patient that needs hope today. You may not have fully understood or experienced everything that you have read in this booklet, but you might sense your own personal need to have a new start in life and receive the promise of eternal life that Jesus offers. Jesus said, "I am come that they might have life, and that they might have *it* more abundantly" (John 10:10). This means that you can have a new start to life, a new way of life, a life that has purpose, meaning, and hope.

Jesus died, was buried, and rose again to give you a new way of life and eternal life with Him forever in Heaven. The Bible tells you how you can receive eternal life and a brand new start in life.

1.   Understand WHO you are.

> Romans 3:23:
> "For all have sinned, and come short of the glory
> of God."

The Bible declares that all of us have sinned against God and have fallen short or missed the mark of God's moral perfection. Are you willing to admit to God that you are a sinner?

2.   Understand WHERE you are going.

> Romans 6:23 says:
> "For the wages of sin *is* death; but the gift of God *is*
> eternal life through Jesus Christ our Lord."

The wages (payment) that we must receive because of our sin is spiritual death or separation from God forever in the judgment of hell. Jesus taught that those who do not have their sins forgiven must suffer the penalty and consequences for their own sins. Revelation 20:15 speaks of the awful fate: "And whosoever was not found written in the book of life was cast into the lake of fire." Sin is what separates us from a holy and righteous God who cannot tolerate sin and sinners in His presence.

3.   Understand WHAT Christ did.

> 1 Peter 2:24:
> "Who his own self bare our sins in his own body
> on the tree" (the cross).

1 Corinthians 15:3-4 gives us the Gospel (good news): "For I delivered unto you first of all that which I also received, how that Christ died for our sins according to the scriptures (paying the penalty or judgment for your sin); And that he was buried (proving the finality of His death), and

that he rose again the third day according to the scriptures: (providing the evidence that the Father received His sacrifice and giving you the hope of eternal life).

Jesus took the wages or the payment of judgment for your own sin upon Himself and now offers to you the free gift of eternal life in exchange ("the gift of God is eternal life through Jesus Christ our Lord" - Romans 6:23).

4.   Understand WHOM you must trust.

> Jesus declared in John 3:15:
> "That whosoever believeth in him should not perish, but have eternal life."

Faith or belief in Christ, which means to place personal trust in His saving provision upon the cross and His resurrection, is the only way to receive the free gift of eternal life. Friend, don't place confidence or trust in yourself. Don't trust anyone or anything else, your church, religious heritage or traditions, or baptism for the salvation of your soul from hell. Transfer your faith to Christ alone since He is the only way to Heaven. In John 14:6 Jesus said, "I am the way, the truth, and the life: no man cometh unto the Father, but by me."

> Ephesians 2:8-9 declares:
> "For by grace (God's kindness through Christ) are ye saved (from hell) through faith (simple trust in Jesus); and that not of yourselves (what we do): *it is* the gift of God (salvation is free!): Not of works (any good things that you have done), lest any man should boast."

Jesus cannot give you eternal life unless you believe or trust in Him to be your only Savior and hope of Heaven.

You don't go to Heaven by default; you go there by decision. A personal response of faith in Christ is required.

Revelation 22:17 says:
"And whosoever will, let him take the water of life freely."

Faith in Christ is likened to taking and drinking a glass of cool and refreshing water. This is because faith involves the appropriation or application of Christ's salvation to your own life. You must personally reach out and take what Christ has to offer to you – salvation from hell and eternal life.

Below is a simple prayer that might help you express faith in Jesus Christ. You can pray it in your own heart and God will hear you and save you "For whosoever shall call upon the name of the Lord shall be saved" (Romans 10:13).

"Dear Lord Jesus, I am a sinner that is separated from Your holy presence. I have never trusted in You to be my Savior. But today I understand that You died upon the cross for me, bearing my own sins and judgment, and then rose again to give me eternal life. Right now I believe in You and Your promise of salvation from hell and eternal life. I transfer my faith to You. I believe that You alone can become my Savior from hell. I thank You for the free gift of salvation, eternal life, and the new start in life that You have given to me today. In Jesus' name, Amen."

When Michael Faraday, the great English physicist, was dying, friends gathered at his bedside. As was often the case in the nineteenth century, they sought some final words from the dying man. "What are your speculations?" they asked. His answer was firm: "Speculations! I have none. I am resting on certainties." The greatest certainty that you can have is to possess eternal life through personal faith in Jesus Christ. And no amount of cancer can reduce the gift of eternal life.

Well, you may have thought that it could never happen to you. But it did! Face it. You have cancer. You must now get over the shock and come to claim these wonderful promises of God's Word. Allow them to permeate your heart, grant you hope, and change your life. Dear friend, you can know that you possess eternal life (1 John 5:13) and you can "find grace to help in time of need" (Heb. 4:16). I trust that you will cling to these precious promises and allow the Holy Spirit to use them in your own life as you battle with cancer. There are many things that cancer cannot do to you!

This booklet has focused on the importance of claiming God's promises as you face cancer. Let's finish by reiterating a special twofold blessing that comes from God's precious promises. Psalm 119:50 speaks of the divine *provision* that God's promises give to us in our time of affliction: "This *is* my comfort in my affliction: for thy word hath quickened me." Psalm 119:92 addresses the divine *protection* that we receive from God's promises in our time of affliction: "Unless thy law *had been* my delights, I should then have perished in mine affliction."

The "exceeding great and precious promises" (2 Peter 1:4) of God's eternal truth, which deal with hope, comfort and strength, are the unchanging things that you need to reflect upon as you fight your battle with cancer. You can't face this trial alone. God and His eternal promises will come to your rescue. "My soul melteth for heaviness: strengthen thou me according unto thy word" (Psalm 119:28).

"God hath not promised skies always blue,
Flower-strewn pathways all our lives through;
God hath not promised sun without rain,
Joy without sorrow, peace without pain.

But God hath promised strength for the day,
Rest for the labor, light for the way,
Grace for the trials, help from above,
Unfailing sympathy, undying love."

— Annie J. Flint, 1919

The promises of God's Word will keep you from experiencing emotional and spiritual defeat. God will not fail you. Tarry at a promise and God will meet you there! God is the God of promise. He keeps His word. God will grant you the grace to stand on the unfailing promises of His eternal Word.

"Standing on the promises of Christ my King,
Thro' eternal ages let His praises ring;
Glory in the highest, I will shout and sing,
Standing on the promises of God.

Standing on the promises that cannot fail,
When the howling storms of doubt and fear assail,
By the living Word of God I shall prevail,
Standing on the promises of God."

— Russell Carter

CPSIA information can be obtained
at www.ICGtesting.com
Printed in the USA
BVHW061925180222
629465BV00007B/130